Crossing the Atlantic

One Family's Story

By Lorraine Jean Hopping

CELEBRATION PRESS
Pearson Learning Group

Contents

Meet the Ferguson Family

The Fergusons are a family of five. They used to live in Miami, Florida. Now their home is a sailboat!

In 2001 the Fergusons began a four-year trip around the world. They wanted to learn about other people and places. This is the story of the first part of the trip—crossing the Atlantic Ocean.

Stephanie

Max

Julia

Maria

Steve

Getting Ready to Go

In 2000 the Fergusons bought their sailboat, the *Dulcinea* (dul-si-NAY-uh). During the next year, the Fergusons turned the boat into a home. They fixed up rooms where they could eat, sleep, and play. They packed food and clothes for months of travel.

The **helm** is the boat's steering equipment.

A boat's kitchen is called a **galley**.

The Fergusons also planned their route across the Atlantic. Weather experts gave the family information about storms forming over the ocean.

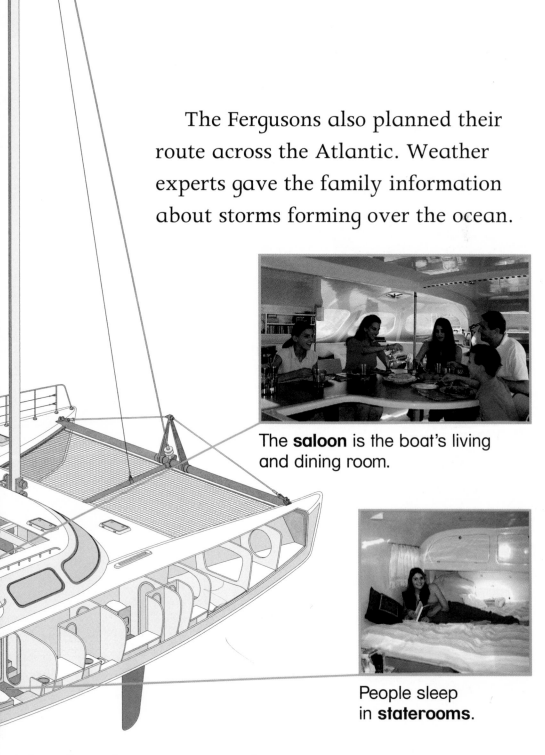

The **saloon** is the boat's living and dining room.

People sleep in **staterooms**.

The Interior of the *Dulcinea*

Setting Sail

On September 8, 2001, the Fergusons **set sail** from the coast of Rhode Island. They did not get far. The next day they found out that a **hurricane** was heading their way! Sailing into such a storm would have been dangerous. So Steve steered the boat back to land.

The Fergusons waited while two more hurricanes passed by. Then, on September 20, the family set sail for the second time. Very strong winds made sailing too difficult, so they had to turn back again.

The Fergusons put on **foul-weather gear** when a storm is approaching. These clothes help keep them warm and dry.

Steve and Max study a map. Maps helped the Fergusons plan their route across the Atlantic.

The family couldn't wait much longer. They needed to start the ocean crossing soon. If they waited, the winter weather would be too rough.

On September 21, the Fergusons set sail for the third time. Two days later yet another hurricane formed. This time the Fergusons sailed around it. They went north, east, and then south across the ocean. This zigzag route made the trip longer, but much safer.

Life at Sea

At sea everyone kept busy. Stephanie, Julia, and Max did their schoolwork onboard the *Dulcinea*. Their mother was their teacher.

sisters doing schoolwork

Everyone had jobs to do. Julia kept the boat neat. Max bagged the garbage. Stephanie steered the boat each night from nine o'clock until midnight while her parents slept. "It got harder to keep my eyes open as the days went by," she said.

Julia storing her schoolbooks

Stephanie on night duty

Julia washing the dishes

Life aboard the *Dulcinea* wasn't all work. The Fergusons also found time for fun. Stephanie watched the sunsets and the stars. Max liked to swing on a bar. Everyone talked, read, and played games.

After nine days, the Fergusons reached the Azores (AY-zors). These are islands about 800 miles west of Spain.

The *Dulcinea* reaches the Azores.

The Fergusons' Ocean Crossing

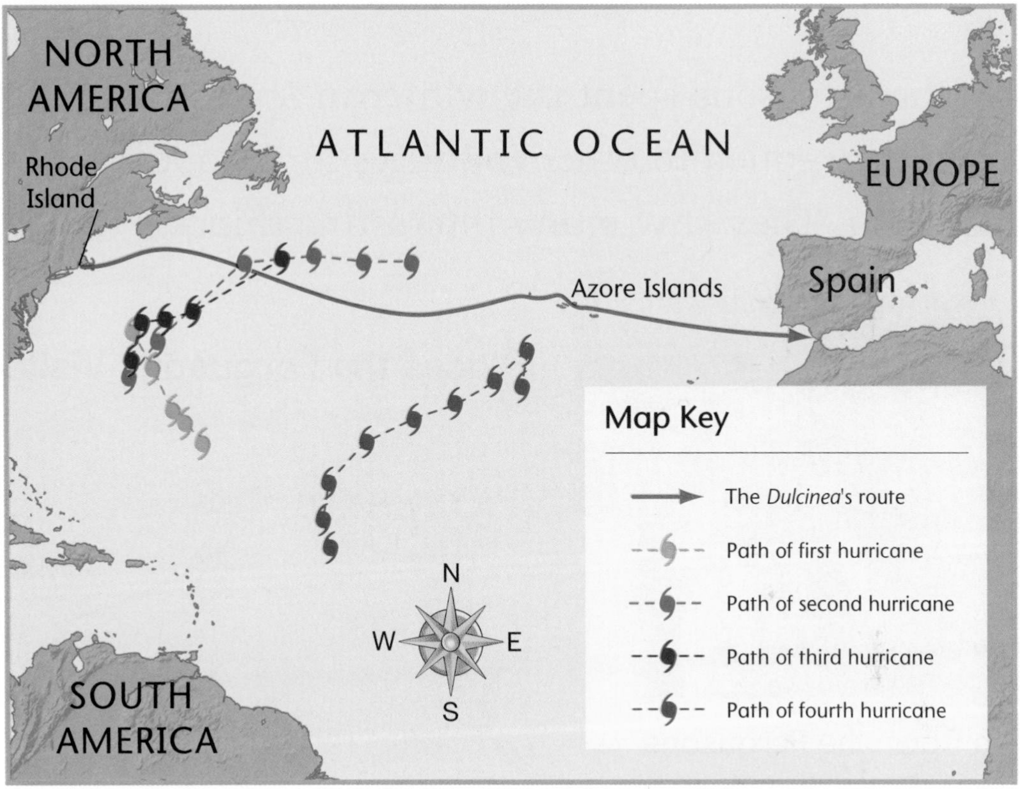
NORTH AMERICA
Rhode Island
ATLANTIC OCEAN
EUROPE
Azore Islands
Spain
SOUTH AMERICA
N
W
E
S
Map Key
The *Dulcinea*'s route
Path of first hurricane
Path of second hurricane
Path of third hurricane
Path of fourth hurricane

People were surprised to see the *Dulcinea*. It was late in the year for a small boat to cross the Atlantic. "What were you doing out there in all that bad weather?" people asked the family.

The Fergusons stayed in the Azores for about three weeks. Then they set sail again. Five days later they landed in Spain. The Fergusons had crossed the Atlantic!

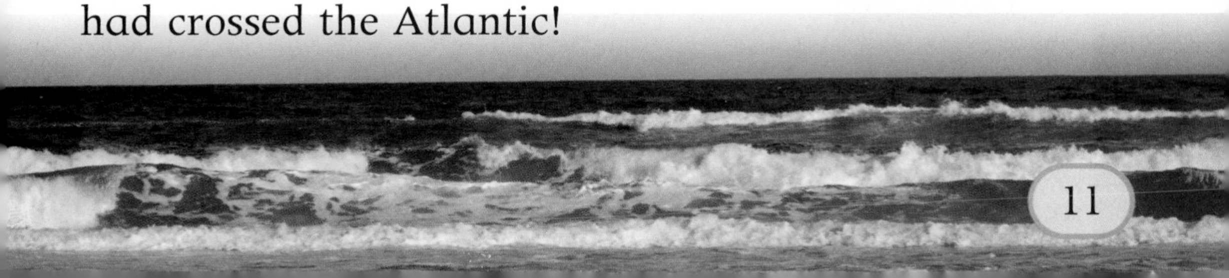

Beyond the Atlantic

The Fergusons spent the winter in Spain. Then they sailed to other countries in Europe and Asia. They saw many interesting things.

In Spain the Fergusons wore Spanish costumes to a festival.

Places the Fergusons Visited

The Fergusons went diving in Spain.

In Greece Steve and Maria steered the *Dulcinea* between tall walls of rock.

In the Mediterranean Sea dolphins swam beside the boat.

EUROPE

Black Sea

Turkey

Greece

terranean Sea

Map Key

→ The *Dulcinea*'s route

In Greece the Fergusons saw some of the sights.

In Turkey Max made new friends, even though he couldn't speak their language.

A year after the journey began, the Fergusons set sail once again. What would they see? Who would they meet? The Ferguson family did not know. Not knowing made them want to go even more.

Author's Note

When I wrote this book in September 2002, I was in the middle of the United States. The Fergusons were sailing in the Black Sea. That's almost halfway around the world!

Even so, reaching the Fergusons was easy. I sent e-mails full of questions. They read the e-mails each time they stopped at a city. The Fergusons also had a cell phone. I called them while they were at sea. I could even hear the waves! I felt like I got to know them—even though I never met them in person.

Author Lorraine Jean Hopping

Glossary

foul-weather gear   clothes worn for protection during bad weather

galley   the kitchen on a boat

helm   the steering equipment on a boat

hurricane   a powerful storm with very strong winds that forms over warm water. Also called a *cyclone*.

saloon   the living and dining room on a boat

set sail   to begin a trip by sailboat

staterooms   bedrooms on a boat